T0145184

ONE *God* OF *Many Names*

The Divine Plan

MICHAEL ALAN KUHN

Balboa Press books may be ordered through booksellers or by contacting:

Balboa Press
A Division of Hay House
1663 Liberty Drive
Bloomington, IN 47403
www.balboapress.com
1 (877) 407-4847

ISBN: 978-1-5043-9415-4 (sc)
ISBN: 978-1-5043-9416-1 (e)

Library of Congress: 2017918983

Print information available on the last page.

Balboa Press rev. date: 12/14/2017

BALBOA.
PRESS
A DIVISION OF HAY HOUSE

DEDICATION

This is dedicated to anyone that wondered why there are so many different religions and if there is one true path to God, heaven, or enlightenment.

One God

Of many names

SECTIONS

INTRODUCTION

I wrote a children's picture book entitled "Why is the Sky Blue?" The characters of the book are cute little animals. I used animal characters to entertain the children and avoid any stereotyping of the characters. The story line has the children resting after playing. They look up to the sky and there are no clouds but just the magnificent blue of the daytime sky. One of the characters asks, "Why the sky is blue?" That evening when each of the little ones was at home they ask their parents, "Why is the Sky Blue?" The next day the children gather to play. When everyone was there they each share the answer their parents offered them. They are very confused as each of their parents had offered a different belief as to why the sky is blue. The children decided to start their own adventure to find an answer to this question.

This book is in tandem with "Why is the Sky Blue." The theme is very similar, in the broad perspective, but the question is, "Why are there so many different religions?" Let's start our own adventure.

It has never felt right to me that any one religion was the true path to enlightenment, salvation, and/or God. I have asked myself these questions:

> If there is a central deity why would there be so many different religions?
> Why would this deity establish so many options for us to pursue and then have only one path be the correct path?

As I began to read about various religions I found that most religions have many characteristics and teachings that are common to all. Almost all religions teach that love is the core to our existence, compassion for others and all things, and provide for guidance for us to be good citizens of society.

As I continued to read about the religions of the world it came to me in a dream that if I viewed each religion as part of the whole, instead of separately, I would see a much more magnificent insight. What if each of the religions of the world are gifts to help us find our way to our personal enlightenment? To me this meant discovering I am one with all and not separate from anyone.

1

Michael Alan Kuhn

I want to take you on my journey. I hope you read this story with an open heart and mind. I have purposely not filled this book with many references to the history of any religion nor have I provided a detained analysis of the teachings of any religion. *To do so would take you away from observing the broad perspective.*

When you look back to when a religion began they generally were filling the need for people in a society to find purpose in life. Most religions also included structure in the form of accepted social behavior that was necessary at the time to bring order and purpose to the society. The teachings of their spiritual leaders created the basis and core for their religion. After the teacher was gone, those coming after made the lessons of these teachers fit the social structure they constructed.

I know many people will want to refute the contents of this book by quoting their religion's holy scripture. I hope you resist the efforts to tear down or criticize what I have presented. Instead focus on the broad perspective to stimulate you looking at your own religion or philosophy with a fresh perspective.

This book is meant to ask you to search your heart as your heart knows the truth. I have made some statements with which you may not agree. You may have a different perspective about what is presented. Wonderful, as there are many layers and perspectives to each person's connection with God. Your personal connection to the Divine is the connection you should honor.

GENERAL OBSERVATIONS

*I*t is common to reference to "God's Plan" when dealing with the unknown. We often offer as an explanation that it is "God's Will" for the things that happen in our life that seem to be random events. We have been told our whole life that we cannot know God's Plan. We accept "God's Will" as we are constantly reminded we must walk with faith and trust in the divine.

What if there is a concept that would assist us to understand and solidify our faith? Instead of any one religion being the path to our enlightenment, what if all the religions of the world are woven together to assist us to find our truth and our place in the Universe.

In this book I am <u>not</u> going to fill the pages with historical facts or references to religious doctrine as it would be counterproductive. There will be others who want to offer their own opinion. Good, as it will open a dialogue that is needed. Read this book with an open heart and mind and see where you find yourself.

If you are offended by what you read because it challenges or contradicts your beliefs, religious teachings, or something else, please read through the entire presentation. Do not stop as it will not take you a long time. You may need to pause periodically to reflect on what you have read. Good, as you are listening to your heart.

HISTORY REVISITED

A new perspective

What if Mother Earth is not the only heavenly body where life exists? What if life forces exist here and in other places and realms in ways that we cannot comprehend? These life forces may have many forms and exist in many different dimensions. This is too complex a topic for this book and can be addressed in the future. Scientists are on the verge of discoveries that will open our minds to new possibilities.

We have all heard the myths about early civilizations of Atlantis or Lumeria. These great societies disappeared as they made the mistake of believing they were more important and powerful than Mother Earth (Gaia). They began to control the elements of Mother Earth and these societies suffered the consequences of their misguided actions. What if these stories are real and life on Mother Earth was in chaos after the fall and destruction of these last great civilization tens of thousands of years ago? Humans had to start over, not from where they were, but start completely anew. The new mankind purposely would have no memory or record of the past civilizations.

The Indigenous Peoples were the custodians of the truth from the beginning and again as the new beginnings were ushered in with the new humanity. The Indigenous Peoples throughout the world became the anchors of human consciousness and the connection to Mother Earth. It is a sacred partnership that is still in force today. Gaia is obviously a living life force but she is much more. She is a life force in co-creation with the Godhead that is not different from each of us and all living things on the planet. She has a soul and a direct connection to the Godhead.

Mankind began to flourish and spread throughout the world. However, mankind languished in darkness which was the price for failure of the previous civilizations. The growth of human consciousness was purposely very slow in a place with so much potential for growth. Life forces from vast reaches of the Universe started dispatching some of their own to assist the evolution (ascension) of mankind and Mother Earth. These emissaries of light were sent to all the continents of Mother Earth. They came to assist in raising the awareness, consciousness, and vibration of mankind and Mother Earth. (Yes, Mother Earth as we are part of her.) These life forces from throughout many Universes assisted mankind and left markers that would peek our curiosity in future generations. The great pyramids and other structures were built with the technological assistance from these visitors. These markers were left to cause the future generations to ask why and plant the seeds within us to seek truth.

These visitors from the stars were limited in the magnitude of assistance and influence they could offer. People had to make all choices of their own free will. Unfortunately, mankind soon became enamored with their visitors and began to idolize them and even make them Gods. For the visitors from the stars this was in direct conflict with their intent and integrity. Therefore, they were required to withdraw in physical form but some were allowed to remain in the energetic field of Mother Earth. (What we call non-physical beings, spirit, unseen friends, ancestors, etc.) This way they could continue to assist but only in this new way through dreams, meditations, and other states of consciousness.

Mankind soon embraced fear as people believed they had done something wrong because their Gods were gone. Mankind created rituals and sacrifices to appease their Gods. These new societies ignored the warnings and teachings of the ones that had departed. They forgot the teachings and examples of the Indigenous People to honor Mother Earth. Mankind lost the understanding of the cycles of Mother Earth and the ways to survive in each cycle. They forgot to honor Mother Earth by protecting her and offering something from themselves whenever they took from her. Just a simple expression of gratitude and honoring all life forces. The result was the decline and subsequent vanishing of these highly evolved societies of Atlantis and Lemuria.

Now what to do?

THE INTRODUCION OF RELIGIONS

TO ASSIST OUR EVOLUTION

*W*hat if *pillars of consciousness for our path to awakening* were introduced to mankind as guidance for its search for the purpose of life? These pillars, in the form of the wisdom and teachings they presented, would be introduced by prophets/teachers from the Godhead in various times and cultures? If these pillars of consciousness were anchored throughout the world, and in every region of the world, the true influence of the divine would be felt by all. Once mankind was able to step back and look at the entire religious teaching of the world there may be an awakening and recognition that we are all one.

There would be no physical contact from members of the Universe. The only contact would be from the non-physical forms of energy and thought sharing. Your soul still knows them and can sense them. Any physical contact would be allowed if requested but contact was limited in its duration.

So how do you get mankind's consciousness to ascend and not make the mistakes of all previous failed civilizations? Each society would be aided by teachers/prophets that would bring forth pillars of consciousness for the path to our awakening for the society to embrace. It is recognized that societies need structure to facilitate some form of order and paths for spiritual growth.

Great teachers emerged from each society and brought forth new messages. The pillar of consciousness from the Godhead that was given to any society by each of these great teachers was unique. Thousands of years ago it would be difficult, all at one time, to be provided with all pillars of consciousness from the Godhead as it could have been overwhelming and not easily comprehended.

What were these gifts to mankind?

Is it possible that if we can see the global intent of the Godhead at work we will become aware of our similarities and less focused on our differences? In addition, if you can see the unique aspect of the pillar of consciousness given to each religion or philosophy, and step back and see the broad perspective, you can see the overall influence of the divine plan. Once you could feel this connection in your heart the thought of peace and serenity will fill you. You will embrace all peoples of all faiths, colors, and beliefs and the Golden Age will be in full bloom.

Instead of debunking the issue(s), why not try to find some form of truth for you in the concept?

Let us explore some of the religions and the unique pillar of consciousness given by the Godhead to each religion. I will not discuss all religions and for those not discussed it does not mean they are less important in representing their gifted aspect from the Godhead. There will be other writers and philosophers who may carry the conversation forward.

INDIGENOUS PEOPLE

*I*ndigenous peoples are any ethic group, with the earliest known historical connection, who have and continue to inhabit a geographic region.

The message brought by all indigenous people is simple. The most important pillar of consciousness for the path of our awakening is to **honor Mother Earth and every living thing.** The indigenous people honor Mother Earth for providing all they need for life and the ability to experience all possibilities. In their honoring of Mother Earth they do nothing to cause harm to their environment. If they take from Mother Earth, such as animals for food, they offer something in return. What the individual offers to Mother Earth is not important as long as the offering does not harm another life force. The sacrifice of a human or animal is not an intended offering. It the intent of the Indigenous People to honor Mother Earth and their action produces harmony throughout the Universe.

No matter where the indigenous people are on Earth, they have the same honor and respect for their home and all the forces of nature they experience. Native Americans offer simple things, like tobacco, in exchange for the gifts they receive from Mother Earth.

It is just this simple. Unfortunately, most of mankind has not recognized this simple truth. I could give you numerous examples but we are all aware of this fact.

We are to stop taking without expressing our gratitude and giving in return.

HINDUISM

Hinduism has no single founder but is a combination of many diverse traditions. I mention it next as it is often called the oldest religion. This religion is complex with many facets.

One of the aspects of the Godhead that is offered in Hinduism is that every action, thought, or decision a person makes has consequences that will return to each person. It sets the foundation of the Godhead's pillar of consciousness for our path to awakening that *we are all co-creators and must take responsibility for our actions*. For many this is known as Karma. It is not a system of punishment but a reminder to take responsibility for our own actions.

Another way to look at this principle was presented many years ago by Dr. James Peebles as he said as one of the principles of life is "Self responsibility for our life as a creative adventure, for though your choices and perceptions you do indeed create your own reality." This is an incredibly powerful statement.

Our mind quickly goes to those people who suffer abuse, oppression, persecution, etc. What was their karma? Throughout history there are wonderful people (like Nelson Mandela) who came from such apparent adverse reality. He survived the dire situation he was in by constantly repeating the last lines of his favorite poem, "I am the master of my fate and the captain of my soul."

There are many paths for people that come from adverse realities once they emerge to a different reality. Some choose to use the adversity to grow, display character, and become humble. Sometimes our reality assists us to experience and find courage, forge our character, and trust in something we cannot explain. Others may carry the experiences of their adverse reality into their new situation and may never emerge from the feelings anchored in during the past difficult times.

What will you do?

JUDAISM

*A*cornerstone to Judaism is the conviction that every human being, simply by virtue of his or her humanity, is a child of God and therefore in procession of the rights that even kings must respect.

Jews are persistent in refusing to see anything innately special about themselves as human beings.

The pillar of consciousness that Jews hold is: ***We are all children of God that must be free.***

The Jews have a long history of captivity and the struggle for freedom which is the desire for all souls. Freedom is the core of every living force on Mother Earth. In Huston Smith's "The illustrated World's Religions" he states, "God at the same time used the Jews to introduce into history insights that all peoples need, but to which they are blinded by complacency. Specifically, God was burning into the Jews through their suffering a passion for freedom and justice that would spread to all mankind."

This may be why Judaism finds holiness and history inseparable.

BUDDHISM

*W*hen Buddha was asked "What are you?" he answered "I am awake." Buddhism begins with a man who woke up. A man determined to follow the calling of a truth-seeker.

Buddhism delivered the pillar of consciousness from the Godhead implanted in us that ***we are all truth seekers.***

The Buddha was not blind to the social side of human nature as he insisted on its importance in reinforcing an individual relationship with themselves and all life. This is the purpose of most world religions. Buddha did not prescribe to a central God but taught that all living things are God.

Buddha reminded everyone of the importance of appealing to the secret workings of the inward heart. This is a reminder that we must not blindly follow the teachings of any religion but must follow our own heart.

Some would describe this as our intuition.

CONFUCIANISM

Confucianism has been considered a philosophy but current scholars consider it to be a religion.

The pillar of consciousness from the Godhead that Confucius brought to us was that *we are all students of the divine and we are also all teachers*.

This levels the playing field as we are all teachers and students and equal. As William Shakespeare wrote; the whole world is a stage and we are all mere actors on this stage of life.

Confucius lived at a time when his society was falling into chaos. His teachings were to aid society to find a base for establishing order and purpose. His passion for this purpose made him a zealot but humor was his way to convey simple principals and kept him from becoming a fanatic.

We learn that trying to impose our beliefs upon another dishonors their individual path to find truth.

CHRISTIANITY

A key to Jesus' teachings was his faith and compassion. He saw and taught that social barriers were an affront to God's compassion. He openly disregarded any social barrier. What Jesus brought to mankind as the pillar of consciousness from the Godhead is the power of **faith and compassion** as he worked to remove social barriers.

The barriers established by mankind were only for conformity to mankind's doctrines or dogma. Jesus taught that everyone should be free of anything that binds or restricts their freedom of choice and their free will.

I realize that others will point to Jesus as being God in human form and describe the miracles he performed as examples of his divinity. Is it possible that the miracles they saw were presented as demonstrations of faith? Jesus did not claim to heal those that were healed – he merely said, "Their faith healed them." Jesus professed that in the future others will do as I do. In the present we often see in the media many examples that demonstration of how people are changed by their faith.

ISLAM

As with all religions of the world, Islam became a religion allowing individuals to follow a doctrine brought forth by the teachings of its founder. Mohammad wanted to return to the principals of biblical teaching before mankind distorted them with its own beliefs. Therefore, Islam embraces the teachings of the old and new testaments with a refreshed and new perspective.

The pillar of consciousness from the Godhead brought forth by Mohammad is the ***return to the core principals of mankind's existence on Mother Earth and to not worship idols as written in all books attributed to God's word.***

Muslims are cautioned against worshipping idols. Buddha, Jesus, and others taught their followers to not idolize them or create shrines to them. However, once they were gone, mankind could not resist and did create many symbols and shrines to memorialize their teachers.

Mohammad insisted that he not be idolized. He wanted the word of God (Allah) and each person's relationship with God to be what brings each person comfort. Statues, figurines, or paintings create an illusion of separation from God.

MYSTIC (NEW AGE)

*T*his is not a religion but the current trend of many individuals returning to mysticism. There have been many mystics over the past centuries, however, the increased interest began to grow after World War II. It cannot be ignored that the flood of "baby boomers" (born after the war) began to search for something different than what they were finding in their houses of worship. The movement grew and became very visible to the world with the harmonic convergence on August 1987. The world began to notice after they saw such a large number of people coming together, on a single date, to recognize a unification of thoughts, desires, and beliefs directed to mankind and Mother Earth. The pillar of consciousness from the Godhead this group of souls brings forth is *acceptance of others, equality, and honoring the feminine.*

A whole group of people were rediscovering and finding new teachers were talking about God and the Universe without ties to any specific religion. It was not just the hippies, flower children, and others any longer. It was the everyday average person starting to question the teachings of the past and searching for a truth that they could not define but knew existed. They were returning to being truth seekers and to follow their heart (intuition).

These individuals were moving away from the dogma of organized religion. They were seeking truth and recognizing the importance of following their heart, gut, or intuition. Women are seen as equals. Women and men are seeking truth and enlightenment. This movement results in a freedom that allowed them to grow while still honoring all their friends and family. The mystic honors the individual path that each person follows.

The acceptance of all people to walk their own truth is best said by Dr. James Peebles in the 1900's when he says, "Loving allowance for all things to be in their right time and place, starting with one's self."

If everyone truly embraced this principle all forms of bias would disappear. I like to describe this as *accepting any path to God is the right path.* There is no one or right path. This is what the characters found in my children's book "Why is the Sky Blue" mentioned in the introduction to this book.

SUMMARY

*I*f you can step back and look at the world and all its diversity, you see the Godhead's fingerprint in everything. Someone asked me, "Why did God create so many different cultures, religions, and societies?" It seems clear that we created all these different experiences in co-creation with the Godhead so we could experience all the aspects of God (ourselves). In these experiences we hopefully become truth seekers which eventually turns to an inward journey. For truth is in your heart.

The great teachers of the last four thousand plus years brought pillars of consciousness from the Godhead that was implanted in human consciousness. It was mankind's choice to take that seed and make it grow. The seed blossomed into the cultures, societies, and religions that have served our needs. It was a way for us to find our way to God and ourselves though the study of the principles and doctrines presented by these great teachers. In this search we eventually go inward and remember we are all an aspect of God, a child of God, and recognize we are not separate from God, and we are all one.

The great teachers of the religions of the world brought forth pillars of consciousness from the Godhead that would guide us during our time on Mother Earth (Gaia). When you look at the sequence of the creation of each religion or society from a broad overview it may make sense. You may see the work of the Divine Plan. You are welcome to find your own perception of the pillar of consciousness from the Godhead in the religions I have presented or any other religion.

The order presented below chronicles the time it was presented to mankind:

Honor Mother Earth	*Indigenous People*
We are all co-creators and must take responsibility for our actions	*Hinduism*
We are all children of God and must be free	*Judaism*
We are all truth seekers	*Buddhism*
We are all students and teachers	*Confucianism*
Faith and compassion	*Christianity*
Return to the foundations of past Teachings without worship idols	*Islam*
Acceptance of others and honoring the feminine	Mystic (new age)

Each great teacher inherited the wisdom and the teachings of the teachers before them. Once a pillar of consciousness from the Godhead is anchored in consciousness it is available to all.

We are all born into a region usually dominated by a specific religion or philosophy. We made this choice for this life to experience what this society offered or the limits it imposed. In the past you would have had to study each religion over time and maybe lifetimes (if you believe in reincarnation). However, with today's technology, in accordance with The Divine Plan, everyone is aware of all these pillars of consciousness, the path to our awakening has quickened, and is becoming stronger beacon in the core of our being.

I know you may be tempted to think or say there is more to the religion(s) than what I have presented. I agree. You are welcome to take the time to research and/or explore each religion. There are many wonderful books on each religion and other books that compare many world religions. I am looking at mankind as having one religion within many cultures celebrating their unique gift from the Godhead. When you look at the religions of the world as a whole it is like looking at a neighborhood and not the individual occupants of each home. When you see the neighborhood (broad picture) it sometime gives you a new perspective.

You could find the way to enlightenment in any religion, culture, or society. However, each religion, culture, and society offers different experiences for the individual. Some of these experiences could be nurturing while others could be repressive. No matter what path you chose you can find the way to enlightenment.

You can then proclaim as Buddha did, "I am awake."

When you view this school called Mother Earth and all she offers, from a broad perspective, you cannot help but to see we are one on the same journey. We are one people of many different colors, beliefs, and experiences. We are one in our pursuit of discovering our divinity. We are not separate from any thing – inanimate or living.

If you can accept this simple premise, then we will find the peace and abundance we all desire.

How about it? Start your own movement to love and honor Mother Earth and everything in, of, or upon it. I would like to close with the beginning to my daily prayers, "Blessed are those on this plane, of this plane, and in this plane (of existence)."

Printed in the United States
By Bookmasters